Embracing
ADVENT

Rediscovering Christmas
in the Chaos

A DAILY DEVOTIONAL

Embracing ADVENT

Rediscovering Christmas
in the Chaos

JEN LUDWIG

Embracing Advent
Copyright © 2021 by Jen Ludwig

Cover Design: 100 Covers
Interior Design: Formatted Books

ISBN #978-0-578-96788-2 (paperback)

CONTENTS

Week 3: Choose JOY

Week 4: LOVE and Be Loved

INTRODUCTION TO ADVENT

Advent means *coming*.

It is a time when we reflect on that moment in history when Jesus *came* into the world as a baby two thousand years ago. It is also a time when we can allow Him to *come* into our hearts in more meaningful ways today.

You may have never heard of Advent. Other than the countdown calendars with twenty-five days' worth of chocolate, it's never crossed your mind.

You may have a liturgical church background. You might be familiar with Advent as a time of solemn contemplation… darkness before light… waiting.

For me, Advent is a time of preparation which provides an opportunity to experience Christmas—the glow of the candles, the celebration of the birth, and the beauty of the story of God using ordinary people in extraordinary ways—for more than a day.

Traditionally, Advent begins the fourth Sunday before Christmas (usually right after Thanksgiving in November) and focuses on four themes:

Week 1 – Hope
Week 2 – Peace
Week 3 – Joy
Week 4 – Love

Over the next four weeks, I invite you to make space to rediscover these gifts as we prepare to celebrate Christmas.

NOTE FROM THE AUTHOR

Hi, my name is Jen.

I am a planner. I *love* to plan. The further in advance, the better. The more detailed, the better. And if I can include color-coded charts? Awesome.

I worked professionally as a product planner for a toy company for years. More recently, I jumped into the travel planning industry. I, unashamedly, have a deep affection for spreadsheets, calendars and budgets.

So, at Christmas, you can imagine… I have elaborate plans. Plans for parties with delicious food paired with perfect playlists. Plans for presents thoughtfully wrapped up with coordinated paper and fabric ribbon. Plans for big, bushy, beautiful, well-lit Christmas trees. Plans for meaningful family prayer times and an Advent season spent fully focusing on Jesus ("the reason for the season"). I make plans for everything to be *just perfect*.

The only problem is… things don't always go according to my plan.

For example, there was the year that our family was rushing home in the chilly evening air from a Christmas Eve service at the beach… My husband accidentally dropped the car keys into the storm drain while trying to load kids and jackets into the car. (Thank God, literally, for the nice waiter at the nearby restaurant who fished them out for us with a hanger.)

Or there was the Christmas that I was about to burst due to the impending arrival of my first child… There was no pretty wrapping paper that year—just a stack of gift bags from Costco that I haphazardly filled while reaching around my enormous belly.

It isn't only lost keys or December due dates that cause stress during the Christmas season. There are a million little things that can shift our attention from the person—Jesus—that we are meant to be celebrating. Universally, there seems to be an annual struggle at this time of year between focusing on what's important and drowning in the busyness.

It is my hope to steer away from the chaos and rediscover the true gifts of Christmas: hope, peace, joy and love.

I did not write this book because I'm good at this balancing act, I wrote it because I'm often terrible at it. I am continually learning how to let go of my own plans and allow God to show me the path and provisions He has for me.

Over the years, I have found that by embracing Advent—a time meant to prepare our hearts for Christmas—I am able to slow down, step away from the stress, and refocus.

And so, these four weeks invite you to follow a different sort of plan… A plan to fully embrace the gifts of hope, peace, joy and love that Jesus offers us.

Instead of thinking about what we will do, or give, or bring to the next holiday party, we will aspire to *Hold on to Hope, Find Peace, Choose Joy,* and *Love and Be Loved.*

It is my prayer that these readings will remind you during this busy time of year that we are not just planning for parties and presents. We are preparing to welcome Jesus into the world and into our hearts.

One last note… Depending on the year, Christmas can fall on any day of the fourth week of Advent. With this in mind, I've included a special note for Christmas Day. No matter which day of the week it falls on, don't miss it—it is a gift for you!

Week One: HOPE

Hold on to Hope

*My prayer is that light will flood your hearts
and that you will understand the hope that
was given to you when God chose you. Then
you will discover the glorious blessings that
will be yours together with all of God's people.*

EPHESIANS 1:18 (CEV)

WEEK ONE: HOPE
Sunday

Waiting with Hope

DURING THE FIRST week of Advent, our focus is on HOPE. Hope implies *waiting*. Hope requires *patience*.

> THE LORD IS GOOD TO THOSE WHO HOPE IN HIM,
> TO THOSE WHO SEEK HIM.
> IT IS GOOD TO WAIT QUIETLY
> FOR THE LORD TO SAVE.
>
> – LAMENTATIONS 3:25-26 (NCV)

The word that is translated as HOPE in these verses is the Hebrew word *qavah*. It is sometimes translated as "to wait for." Its literal definition is "to bind together (perhaps by twisting)"[1] and comes from the word for *cord*.

The word means, in essence, the feeling of anticipation you have when you are waiting for something positive to happen. *Qavah* can be compared to the secure tension you feel when you are holding onto a rope and someone else is also holding firmly to the other end of it. In my mind, I picture a strong, braided rope holding us fast to God.

Imagine what happens when you let go of the rope or allow too much slack… no more tension. No more hope.

In other words, hope requires some action on our part.

Waiting quietly might not seem like an action. In fact, for someone like me (replete with checklists and star charts), waiting seems very much like total *inaction*.

Yet, this is how we are called to hope. In order to actively *find* hope, *hold on to* hope, *cling to* hope, and *be anchored in* hope; we actually need to be very deliberate in our patient waiting.

Waiting quietly cannot happen as we run from place to place and bake, shop, sing, and eat our way through the holiday season.

Waiting quietly requires time, a place where we will not be disturbed, and listening ears to discover the small steps God has put in front of us for this day, instead of rushing ahead to the finish line on our own.

And as we patiently wait with anticipation, God promises to strengthen us…

BUT THOSE WHO HOPE [QAVAH] IN THE LORD
WILL RENEW THEIR STRENGTH.
THEY WILL SOAR ON WINGS LIKE EAGLES;
THEY WILL RUN AND NOT GROW WEARY,
THEY WILL WALK AND NOT BE FAINT.

– ISAIAH 40:31 (NIV)

I invite you this Advent season, as you start making your to-do lists, to carve out time to *wait quietly*. Intentionally set aside still moments to seek Him. Find a comfy chair and have a one-on-one conversation with God for a few minutes each day. Hold on to the rope of HOPE—and feel what it is like to find Him holding on securely to the other end.

WEEK ONE: HOPE
Monday

Looking Forward with Hope

WHAT IS FAITH?
IT IS THE CONFIDENT ASSURANCE THAT SOMETHING
WE WANT IS GOING TO HAPPEN.
IT IS THE CERTAINTY THAT WHAT WE HOPE
FOR IS WAITING FOR US,
EVEN THOUGH WE CANNOT SEE IT UP AHEAD.

– HEBREWS 11:1 (TLB)

FAITH IS BEING confident that what we hope for is waiting for us…
even if we can't see it yet.

But *how* can we be so confident?

We can be confident in the future by looking back at the past. We look
forward with hope by looking *back* at God's faithfulness to us.

Hebrews 11 goes on to list heroes of the Old Testament and recount the ways that God was faithful to them in the most implausible circumstances...

> *Noah was told to build a boat in the middle of the desert. And because of his faithfulness, his family was spared from the flood.*

> *God told Abraham that his barren wife, Sarah, would have a child and that his descendants would outnumber the grains of sand along the seashore. And his 90-year-old wife gave birth to Isaac.*

> *Moses' mother defied the Egyptian decree to kill the Israelite babies and set her child afloat down the Nile river in a basket. And He would later rise to prominence in Egypt and lead his people to freedom.*

Reading these stories helps us to look forward with hope by looking back at the times that God has been faithful.

How do *you* remember God's faithfulness?

Our Christmas tree is a mishmash of ornaments. You would think that someone with my affection for order would have one of those Christmas trees that stand in a department store window—a theme of white lights and red balls, or carefully curated porcelain bells with soft silver tinsel. Instead, our tree holds an array of curious baubles and keychain charms that mark the memories of various travels, special family moments, and childhood memories.

There is an ornament for each of my 23 anniversaries with my husband—a seashell from our five-year anniversary in Jamaica, a little surfboard from our weekend in Newport Beach, a snowman from our trip to Chicago.

There is an ornament for each Christmas we've had with our kids, themed with whatever activity or obsession dominated that year—a silver rattle the year my daughter was born, a Hallmark Hot Wheels ornament for the year my son was passionate about little toy cars, glass-blown passports for the year we traveled throughout Europe.

Filling the spaces in-between are countless ornaments from trips with friends and family, a few faded treasures from my own childhood, and a sprinkling of the *12 Days of Christmas* Disney ornaments my in-laws gave us before we had so many wonderful mementos to fill our tree.

When I look at that tree, I am amazed at all the precious memories our little family has stored up over the past couple of decades… and I look forward to the additions that will inevitably adorn our future Christmas trees.

In the same way, we need to store up our collection of memories of God's faithfulness. We need to treasure these remembrances, then pull them out every once in a while to remind ourselves of all He has done and hold on to the hope that He will continue to be faithful to us.

What are the ways you've seen God work in your life in the past? I encourage you to take note of the times He has answered your prayers… the times that you've seen Him open doors that could not open on their own… the times that He has been faithful to you… and keep them in a journal.

This Advent season, if you are feeling concerned that you cannot see what is up ahead—*look back*. Look back, just as the author of Hebrews did, and let God's past faithfulness give you confidence and HOPE in your future.

WEEK ONE: HOPE
Tuesday

Hope Together

HAVE YOU EVER handed someone a gift on Christmas Day, but they refused it when you tried to give it to them?

I can't even imagine carefully choosing presents for my family, wrapping them up with bows, and placing them under the tree—just to have everyone ignore the boxes on Christmas morning.

As we spend time this Advent season discovering the gifts God offers to us, we need to imagine our Father kindly handing them to us. And then, we need to *receive* them.

One of the gifts he extends to us is HOPE. Hebrews 10 says that we should not just accept, but *hold tightly* to, the hope that God offers us.

LET US HOLD TIGHTLY WITHOUT WAVERING
TO THE HOPE WE AFFIRM,
FOR GOD CAN BE TRUSTED TO KEEP HIS PROMISE.
LET US THINK OF WAYS TO MOTIVATE ONE ANOTHER TO
ACTS OF LOVE AND GOOD WORKS.
AND LET US NOT NEGLECT OUR MEETING TOGETHER,
AS SOME PEOPLE DO,
BUT ENCOURAGE ONE ANOTHER,
ESPECIALLY NOW THAT THE DAY OF HIS
RETURN IS DRAWING NEAR.

– HEBREWS 10:23-25 (NLT)

But how do we hold tightly to this hope? The advice in these verses is to hold on to hope by spending time with others so that we can encourage one another.

It is hard to have hope alone. God knows that we need one another, which is why we are designed to be in community together. Right at the start of the Bible, it says in Genesis that it is not good for man to be alone (Genesis 2:18 ESV). Whether it is in our marriages, families, friendships or churches, we are meant to meet together, motivate one another and encourage each other in our faith. We are supposed to remind each other that God can be trusted to keep his promises.

What are your plans this Christmas season? Have you included opportunities to gather with others to encourage each other in the hope that we have in Jesus? In this particularly hectic season, it is important that we do not neglect meeting together. We need to be there for one another to remind others (and ourselves!) that we have HOPE.

This Advent season, carve out a little time to get together with others to motivate and encourage one another. Maybe you can...

Gather with a small group of friends for prayer and encouragement before tackling your to do list.

Join a church or community Christmas choir and sing songs that bring hope.

Attend a Christmas Eve service where you can celebrate Jesus' birth with others. (If you do not regularly attend a local church, don't be shy to visit someplace new!)

Choose to be a part of God's larger church family, knowing that your presence matters. Bring encouragement to someone... and receive encouragement from being together. Dig deeper into your community of believers. Let's hold tightly—together!—to the HOPE we've been promised!

WEEK ONE: HOPE
Wednesday

Hope in God's Promises

WHEN WE READ the Christmas story, our focus is primarily on the account of Jesus' birth as it is told in the New Testament (particularly in the gospels of Matthew and Luke). We marvel at the faith and obedience of Joseph and Mary as they are told that Jesus will be born, and then have the joy of experiencing his miraculous arrival nine months later.

Yet, we need to remember that these promises were not first made to Jesus' parents. The promise of Jesus' birth was initially made hundreds of years before, as foretold in the Old Testament…

> *Those who walked in the dark*
> *have seen a bright light.*
> *And it shines upon everyone*
> *who lives in the land*
> *of darkest shadows.*

A child has been born for us.
We have been given a son
    who will be our ruler.
His names will be
Wonderful Advisor
    and Mighty God,
Eternal Father
    and Prince of Peace.
His power will never end;
    peace will last forever.
He will rule David's kingdom
    and make it grow strong.
He will always rule
    with honesty and justice.
The Lord All-Powerful
    will make certain
    that all of this is done.
– Isaiah 9:2, 6-7 (CEV)

Jesus Christ is the fulfillment of a promise—God's promise to send a Messiah to save His people. Those walking in darkness had been waiting for Christ's light to come into the world for *generations*. There were many who were not able to see God's promise fulfilled in their lifetimes… yet it did come to pass.

Sometimes, we are discouraged when we do not see our short-term hopes fulfilled. Whether it be for a job, a relationship, or even a Christmas gift—hope's anticipation can quickly turn to disappointment.

HOPE DEFERRED MAKES THE HEART SICK,
BUT A LONGING FULFILLED IS A TREE OF LIFE.

– PROVERBS 13:12 (NIV)

Life sometimes defers our hopes and plans, which leaves us aching. However, the hope and life that God promises for our future—in His timing—for restoration (Acts 3:21 NIV)… for justice (Isaiah 30:18 NIV)… for no more tears (Revelation 21:4 NIV)… can be trusted.

And the hope that He offers us for today—that He will be with us always (Matthew 28:20 NIV)… that He carries us (Isaiah 46:4 NIV)… that He offers us freedom (John 8:36 NIV)… can be trusted.

Jesus has fulfilled, is fulfilling, and will fulfill all of God's promises.

FOR ALL OF GOD'S PROMISES HAVE BEEN FULFILLED
IN CHRIST WITH A RESOUNDING "YES!"
AND THROUGH CHRIST, OUR "AMEN" (WHICH MEANS
"YES") ASCENDS TO GOD FOR HIS GLORY.

– 2 CORINTHIANS 1:20 (NLT)

We may not have the privilege of seeing all of God's promises fulfilled in our lifetime (though we give Him great praise when we do!) but know this… The promises that God has made us, He will keep. And this is why we have HOPE.

This Christmas, may we hold on to the HOPE that has already been fulfilled in Christ, the hope that He offers us today, and the hope He promises for our future and let us say, "Amen!"

WEEK ONE: HOPE
Thursday

Hope in His Word

HOPE IS NOT observable. It is abstract. Although not physical, it involves both the head and the heart. Hope is something we feel at our core, but more than just a fleeting feeling, it is rooted in a deep-seated knowledge and confidence.

When we are feeling lost and are searching for hope, it can be elusive. But the Psalmist tells us exactly where to find hope...

> YOU ARE MY HIDING PLACE AND MY SHIELD;
> I HOPE IN YOUR WORD.
>
> – PSALM 119:114 (ESV)

When I was in high school, I worked at a summer camp in Northern California. During a season when I was just starting to spend time reading my Bible on my own, I would go out to the meadow early every morning and sit on the fence along a horse corral, looking out toward the sun rising behind the mountains. I had no idea where to begin, but a co-worker suggested that I simply read through the Psalms and note what I discovered about who God is.

So, I would sit on that fence with my student Bible and open my notebook, and I would read…

> *I love you, O LORD, my strength.*
> *The LORD is my rock and my fortress and my deliverer,*
> *my God, my rock, in whom I take refuge,*
> *my shield, and the horn of my salvation, my stronghold.*
> *I call upon the LORD, who is worthy to be praised*
> *and I am saved from my enemies.*
> – Psalm 18:1-3 (ESV)

And then I would write.

God is…
… my strength.
… my rock.
… my fortress.
… my deliverer.
… my God.
… my shield.
… my salvation.
… my stronghold.
… my Lord.
… worthy to be praised.
… my savior.

And there I would find hope. Reading through the Psalms, and learning more about God and His character, brought assurance to my head and comfort to my heart.

Today, I encourage you to open a Bible and discover more about who God is and the hope that He brings. Get to know Him better through the Psalms, read the Christmas story of Jesus' birth in the books Matthew and Luke, or dive into Romans to learn more about the "good news" of the gospel. The Bible is a gift to us, and in it are accounts and encounters that bring truth and life and HOPE.

WEEK ONE: HOPE
Friday

Hope Amidst Grief

DURING THIS HOLIDAY season, many of us face sadness. In fact, even if things are going really well in our lives, for many people, the holidays have a way of resurfacing all kinds of past pain.

Maybe you are missing a loved one who will not be with you this Christmas or are mourning a relationship that has been fractured or broken. Maybe the family gatherings are difficult for you, or perhaps you feel left out in the cold when others come together to celebrate.

When we consider HOPE, we often think of a positive outlook. We suppose that having hope means looking at the future with expectation, without being affected by the difficult things surrounding us. We believe that hope is a feeling that should erase sadness, instead of an emotion to come alongside it.

In the book of John, we find the story of Jesus raising his friend Lazarus from the dead. And it is here that we find the shortest verse in the Bible... just before Jesus rolls the stone away from Lazarus' tomb:

JESUS WEPT.

– JOHN 11:35 (ESV)

We do not know exactly why He wept, except that He was deeply moved.

Perhaps He wept in sorrow in the presence of death, a symptom of a fallen world. Perhaps He wept in sympathy for his friends Mary and Martha as they mourned the passing of their brother. Perhaps He wept because a tragedy needed to occur for a miracle to happen. But this verse is clear... Jesus was moved to tears.

And here is what strikes me... Jesus wept—even knowing that, just moments later, he would raise Lazarus from the dead! Jesus wept during his grief and sadness, *even as He had hope.*

The God of the universe, fully aware that this situation would be resolved in moments, fully aware that the story was not over, fully aware that good was just around the corner... wept.

Whatever situation you find yourself in this season, God sees you in your grief. He is *deeply moved.* In fact, I believe that He weeps with you today, just as He wept with his friends.

And He offers HOPE. Hope that the story is not over. Hope in an outcome you could not predict. Hope that life and miracles can come from death and darkness. Hope that you are not alone in your tears.

THE LORD IS THERE TO RESCUE
ALL WHO ARE DISCOURAGED
AND HAVE GIVEN UP HOPE.

– PSALM 34:18 (CEV)

This Advent season, if you find yourself discouraged, let Jesus sit with you in your grief, weep with you in your sadness, and comfort you in your pain. He shares in your suffering today even as He knows what lies ahead and offers HOPE.

WEEK ONE: HOPE
Saturday

Hope of Salvation

WHILE GOD DOES not promise that our lives will be free from trouble, He *does* promise us protection as we face life's battles.

There are a few places where the Bible talks about the *armor of God*. The most commonly referenced passage is Ephesians 6 (which we'll look at next week). There is also mention of an important helmet in 1 Thessalonians 5...

> BUT SINCE WE BELONG TO THE DAY,
> WE MUST STAY ALERT AND CLEARHEADED
> BY PLACING THE BREASTPLATE OF FAITH AND LOVE
> OVER OUR HEARTS,
> AND A HELMET OF THE HOPE OF SALVATION
> OVER OUR THOUGHTS.
>
> – 1 THESSALONIANS 5:8 (TPT)

We need the helmet of the HOPE of salvation on our heads because *our anxious thoughts lead us away from hope*. When we let our minds wander and focus on our present-day difficulties, instead of focusing on the One who is Lord over all, we lose sight of the eternal promises we've been given through Jesus.

Consider the story of Peter walking on water… Jesus calls for him to come out on the water…

> *So Peter went over the side of the boat and walked on the water toward Jesus. But when he saw the strong wind and the waves, he was terrified and began to sink.* – Matthew 14:29-30 (NLT)

As soon as Peter takes his eyes off Jesus and starts looking around him, he begins to falter. So, how do we keep our eyes from wandering when life is difficult? How do we put on hope as a helmet to protect ourselves from our anxious thoughts?

There are a number of ways that we can remind ourselves of the certain HOPE we can have…

> We can read God's word, where we find our hope. (Ps. 119 ESV)

> We can go to the Lord in prayer, who promises to hear us and give us hope. (Jeremiah 29:11-12 ESV)

> We can surround ourselves with a community of Christian believers that will support and encourage us as we put our hope in our salvation. (1 Thessalonians 5:8-11 ESV)

Some days, however, we might feel like the wind and waves are too big to ignore. There are still times when we lose our focus, just like Peter…

> *But when he saw the strong wind and the waves, he was terrified and began to sink. "Save me, Lord!" he shouted. Jesus immediately reached out and grabbed him.* – Matthew 14:30-31 (NLT)

I love that Jesus was right there to catch him. And I think that is part of the "hope of salvation"—knowing that, when we put our trust in Jesus, He will be there to catch us, too.

This Advent season, no matter what is pulling you away from hope, try not to let yourself be distracted by the wind or waves around you. Be clearheaded, protect your head with the helmet He offers, and keep your thoughts focused on the HOPE we have in Christ. Jesus' birth was just the beginning of the story of God coming to dwell with us and die for us so that we can hold on to the HOPE of salvation.

Week Two: PEACE

Find Peace

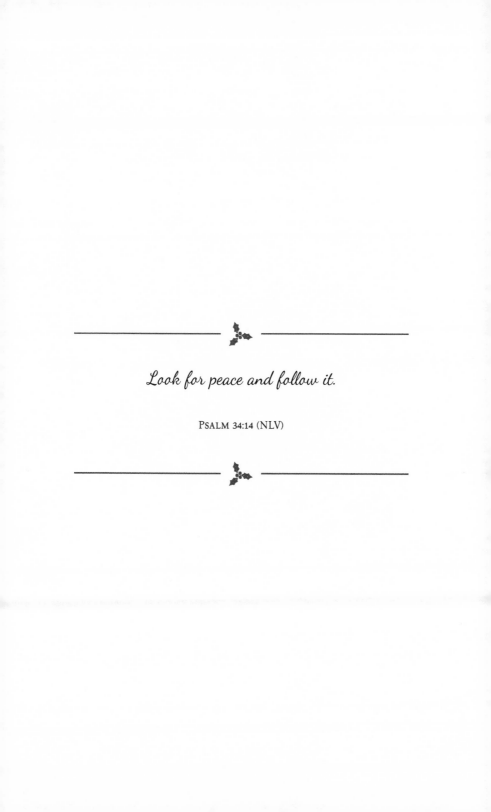

Look for peace and follow it.

PSALM 34:14 (NLV)

WEEK TWO: PEACE
Sunday

Trade Worry for Peace

THERE IS A story in the Bible of Jesus visiting the home of two sisters…

> *As they continued their journey, Jesus came to a village and a woman called Martha welcomed him to her house. She had a sister by the name of Mary who settled down at the Lord's feet and was listening to what he said. But Martha was very worried about her elaborate preparations and she burst in, saying, "Lord, don't you mind that my sister has left me to do everything by myself? Tell her to get up and help me!"*
>
> *But the Lord answered her, "Martha, my dear, you are worried and bothered about providing so many things. Only a few things are really needed, perhaps only one. Mary has chosen the best part and you must not tear it away from her!"*
>
> – Luke 10:38-42 (PHILLIPS)

I am a "Martha."

I have already admitted that I am an avid planner, overflowing with an abundance of ideas just waiting to be put into action. Particularly for a holiday. Or a birthday. Or, for the sake of our purposes here, Christmas.

My elaborate preparations during these weeks leading up to December 25th can bring a lot of joy, community, and gifts… along with unachievable expectations, sleep deprivation, and stress.

It took me some years (and tears) to realize that I have a choice to make as I prepare for Christmas. I can, like Martha, be "worried and bothered about providing so many things" or I can take the opportunity to sit and soak in the story, once again, of Jesus coming to the world in the form of a babe out of His great love for us.

And here's the best part… By choosing *not* to worry—and opting instead to meet with God in prayer—we are promised PEACE.

DO NOT BE ANXIOUS ABOUT ANYTHING,
BUT IN EVERY SITUATION,
BY PRAYER AND PETITION, WITH THANKSGIVING,
PRESENT YOUR REQUESTS TO GOD.
AND THE PEACE OF GOD, WHICH TRANSCENDS
ALL UNDERSTANDING,
WILL GUARD YOUR HEARTS AND YOUR MINDS IN CHRIST JESUS.

– PHILIPPIANS 4:6-7 (NIV)

This verse encourages us to bring our worries to God in *every* situation. Whether you are concerned about the elaborate preparations you find yourself overseeing (at home, the office or school), or how you are going to afford Christmas gifts, or what the celebration will look like without someone you love at the table this year... remember that nothing is too big or too small to take to Him. Although we can feel pulled to plan and prepare and handle those things on our own, Jesus invites us to sit at His feet, give our anxieties over to Him in prayer, and let the overwhelming PEACE of God fill our hearts.

As I continue to soak in this truth, I am learning to not get so consumed with my plans that I lose sight of their purpose. At the same time, I am learning to embrace the planner in me, and I am increasingly confident that this is who God purposefully made me.

I still plan for parties and gather everyone up for family movies and spend hours choosing the perfect gifts so that I can decoratively wrap them with love. But when those detailed preparations start to unravel and cause me to be worried and bothered—and distracted from the goal of *who* we are celebrating—I will choose to find peace at Jesus' feet.

This week, I invite you to do the same. While you may not be able to abandon all of your plans and preparations, I encourage you to reflect on the *purpose* of your Christmas undertakings. Then, with a thankful heart, bring any anxieties you have to Jesus through prayer, and let Him give you PEACE.

WEEK TWO: PEACE
Monday

He is Our Peace

Silent night, holy night
All is calm, all is bright
Round yon Virgin, Mother and Child
Holy Infant, so tender and mild
Sleep in heavenly peace
Sleep in heavenly peace

"SILENT NIGHT" IS a traditional carol that we often hear throughout the Christmas season. Its simple lyrics and beautiful melody bring to mind an image of incredible peace and tranquility.

But, if I'm being honest, I've always struggled a bit with this song.

When I imagine the scene of a teenage mother, away from her home and her family, going through the pains of childbirth in a smelly stable, it hardly brings to mind an image of *peace*.

For many of us, it is the same today. We hear the carol play on the radio as we sit in traffic, in stores as we fight the crowds, at the office as we struggle to meet year-end deadlines, or in our homes as we frantically address Christmas cards... and the season feels anything but peaceful.

And yet...

God promises us PEACE. Peace in *any* place and *any* circumstance.

> FOR HE HIMSELF IS OUR PEACE.
>
> – EPHESIANS 2:14 (ESV)

For *He himself* is our peace.

Peace is not the absence of struggle. Peace is the presence of *someone*... Jesus.

Someone who promises to be with us always. (Matthew 28:20 ESV)
Someone who promises abundant life. (John 10:10 ESV)
Someone who promises to love us unconditionally. (Rom. 8:38-39 ESV)

If we try to find peace in our circumstances, we discover that they are always changing, so our peace is not consistent. There will always be physical pain, financial difficulty, and even war and political unrest in our world. If we think we can only have peace in the absence of these circumstances, we will always be wanting. For one thing is certain, we will not navigate through this life without facing hardships.

Yet in the midst of this ever-changing world, God invites us to anchor our peace in an unchanging person. A lesser known refrain from a later verse of "Silent Night" reminds us...

> *Jesus, God's promise for peace*
> *Jesus, God's promise for peace*[2]

Just as it was that first Christmas, I pray that you can find heavenly peace in the middle of whatever your own smelly stable/unforeseen family change/unexpected surroundings are today. While circumstances may change, God does not. And HE is our PEACE.

WEEK TWO: PEACE
Tuesday

Live Together in Peace

WHAT DOES IT mean to be a peacemaker? The apostle Paul says to the Ephesians:

> FINALLY, BROTHERS AND SISTERS, REJOICE! STRIVE
> FOR FULL RESTORATION, ENCOURAGE ONE ANOTHER,
> BE OF ONE MIND, LIVE IN PEACE. AND THE GOD
> OF LOVE AND PEACE WILL BE WITH YOU.
>
> – 2 CORINTHIANS 13:11 (NIV)

Peace—or *shalom*—in the Old Testament refers not just to the absence of conflict, but to the process of something being made complete or whole. And so, as much as it is in our control, we should also pursue this wholeness in our families and in our communities so that we might live in peace.

We are called to *strive for full restoration*. This is not about just tolerating each other or living free from (or avoiding) conflict. This means moving toward reconciliation and restoration within our families, friendships, and communities—which can also be painful and difficult. Full restoration seems like a tall order, but what I love is that our calling is simply to *strive* for this. We should not be paralyzed into inaction by fearing that we bear the full responsibility for peace. We may not be able to bring peace to every situation on our own, but we are called to make every effort to bring healing where we are able, to "do better"[3] and work together with others to bring restoration.

We are called to *encourage one another*. Part of being a peacemaker means seeing the best in everyone and every situation—and calling it out. Our words have the ability to build others up or tear them down. (And I would argue that encouraging others benefits *us* as much as it benefits the person we are encouraging.) Finding peace in relationships often requires us to focus on what we have in common, the gifts that God has given each of us, and our collective contributions.

We are called to *be of one mind*. Even in my house, with only four humans living under one roof, I know that we cannot agree to "be of one mind" on many things! I prefer the biblical translations which say, "live in harmony with one another." As a singer, I understand harmony to include *different* voices and melody lines in a way that works together to create something beautiful!

And as we do our best to be peacemakers… the God of peace will be with us. He will fill in the gaps and bring us closer to being complete, mature, and whole.

I pray that this Advent season, you will be drawn closer to wholeness and completeness, embracing the peace that God offers. And, in turn, I pray you can bring someone in your inner circle or your larger community closer to wholeness as well. As you set your mind on the PEACE of God, consider how you can strive for reconciliation in a relationship, encourage someone who needs reassurance, or work in harmony to bring community restoration today.

WEEK TWO: PEACE
Wednesday

Peace Shoes

THROUGHOUT THE BIBLE, we often see that having peace is closely tied to resting in God's strength (instead of our own).

> THE LORD GIVES STRENGTH TO HIS PEOPLE;
> THE LORD BLESSES HIS PEOPLE WITH PEACE.
>
> – PSALM 29:11 (NIV)

When we look at *how* we can be "strong in the Lord," we are encouraged to put on the full armor of God...

> FINALLY, BE STRONG IN THE LORD AND IN HIS MIGHTY POWER...
> STAND FIRM THEN, WITH THE BELT OF TRUTH BUCKLED
> AROUND YOUR WAIST, WITH THE BREASTPLATE OF
> RIGHTEOUSNESS IN PLACE, AND WITH YOUR FEET FITTED WITH
> THE READINESS THAT COMES FROM THE GOSPEL OF PEACE.
> IN ADDITION TO ALL THIS, TAKE UP THE SHIELD OF FAITH,
> WITH WHICH YOU CAN EXTINGUISH ALL THE FLAMING ARROWS

OF THE EVIL ONE. TAKE THE HELMET OF SALVATION AND THE
SWORD OF THE SPIRIT, WHICH IS THE WORD OF GOD. AND
PRAY IN THE SPIRIT ON ALL OCCASIONS WITH ALL KINDS OF
PRAYERS AND REQUESTS. WITH THIS IN MIND, BE ALERT AND
ALWAYS KEEP ON PRAYING FOR ALL THE LORD'S PEOPLE.

– EPHESIANS 6:10, 14-18 (NIV)

I'm a visual learner. Passages like this help me to practically picture
what I need to do each day… buckle truth around my waist, put on a
breastplate of Jesus' righteousness (not my own!), and slip on my shoes
of peace for a start.

I imagine that "peace shoes" would help us to walk gently… not with
loud and clunky feet that would draw attention to ourselves, but shoes
that would help us to tread lightly as we interact humbly with the
world around us.

I imagine that "peace shoes" would protect us when we're walking
through rough spots… making sure our feet were covered, especially
in the times we need to pass through deep valleys, prickly thorns, or
broken glass.

I imagine that "peace shoes" would be equipped with sturdy soles to
keep us from slipping and allow us to go the extra mile… giving us
perseverance that we could not manage barefoot.

Our "peace shoes" are also associated with *readiness*. That makes sense
to me—especially thinking back to when my kids were young. Our
family might be just about to walk out the door, but then there would
be a last-minute scramble when everyone was trying to find, put on, or

tie their shoes. We were not ready to leave the house until everybody's shoes were on! So, it's logical to me that we need to *already* have our peace shoes on before difficulty or conflict or trouble arrives, so we are equipped and prepared.

I'm not sure what your "peace shoes" would look like—slippers, hiking boots, or something a little more stylish—but I encourage you to find them and slip them on every morning this Advent season. Take a moment when you get dressed each day to ask God to give you *His* strength so that you are ready to face the day with PEACE.

WEEK TWO: PEACE
Thursday

Prince of Peace

AS WE MOVE through this week's theme of peace, we cannot overlook the Old Testament prophecy about Jesus, where we find that he is referred to as the *Prince of Peace*.

> FOR TO US A CHILD IS BORN,
> TO US A SON IS GIVEN,
> AND THE GOVERNMENT
> WILL BE ON HIS SHOULDERS.
> AND HE WILL BE CALLED
> WONDERFUL COUNSELOR,
> MIGHTY GOD,
> EVERLASTING FATHER,
> PRINCE OF PEACE.
>
> – ISAIAH 9:6 (NIV)

"Prince of Peace" is no small title. It implies royalty and majesty. Rulership and sovereignty. Mandate and authority.

When Jesus arrived on the scene and began his ministry, many of his followers assumed that the Prince of Peace had come to finally rule over a worldly kingdom. They envisioned Him overthrowing the Roman government and reigning on an earthly throne.

But His plans were far greater than they could have imagined.

How hard it must have been for his disciples to understand that their Prince... the one whose Father was the living God, the one who had all authority to be seated on the throne over heaven and earth, the one they thought would topple the cruel Roman rulers... chose not to forcefully take His rightful throne, but instead humbled himself and gave His life on a cross.

But Jesus knew that in order for His people—His sons and daughters that He loved—to have true peace, they needed something more. They needed to be reconciled to a new relationship with their King. They needed the Prince of Peace to bridge the gap between a broken people and a Holy God.

As Prince of Peace, Jesus desires to bring restoration, reconciliation, and peace to our relationships... with our Heavenly Father, with our family and friends, and within our communities.

As you reflect this Christmas on Jesus coming to the world as the Prince of Peace, consider if there is any area you need to give Him authority in your life. Is there a relationship that you think He cannot repair? Is there a habit you think He cannot help you break? Is there a hurt you think He cannot heal? Close your eyes and imagine Him sitting on the throne... reigning over the areas of your heart, mind and soul that are crying out for true PEACE.

WEEK TWO: PEACE
Friday

Jesus Gives Us Peace

THIS CRAZY WORLD gives us our fair share of trouble... Wars. Disasters. Disease. Division. Difficult relationships. Challenging jobs. Global pandemics.

Fortunately for us, *Jesus does not give as the world gives.* Instead, Jesus gives us a helper.

"THE HELPER IS THE HOLY SPIRIT.
THE FATHER WILL SEND HIM IN MY PLACE.
HE WILL TEACH YOU EVERYTHING
AND HELP YOU REMEMBER EVERYTHING I HAVE TOLD YOU.
PEACE I LEAVE WITH YOU. MY PEACE I GIVE TO YOU.
I DO NOT GIVE PEACE TO YOU AS THE WORLD GIVES.
DO NOT LET YOUR HEARTS BE TROUBLED OR AFRAID."

– JOHN 14:26-27 (NLV)

God sends a *helper* who brings us peace. The word summed up as "helper" in this verse can also be translated as *comforter, advocate, intercessor, counselor,* or *strengthener.*[4]

As you face trouble in this world, I want to remind you that you have a *comforter* to soothe your pain, an *advocate* to represent you, an *intercessor* to speak for you, a *counselor* to guide you, and a *strengthener* to support you.

I have come before God in prayer on countless occasions and asked for the Holy Spirit to work in each of these ways. I have brought my hurt and sadness to him. I have asked for direction when making difficult decisions. I have pleaded for strength when I have felt too physically or emotionally spent to get through one more day. I have cried out in frustration when I did not know where to begin.

Sometimes I walk away from those times of prayer with immediate remedies… sorrow lifted, path clear, energy restored. Other times, I am asked to wait. But, even in that waiting, I am promised a companion to be with me in my time of need. And that knowledge… that awareness that I am not alone… that assurance of a helper to help carry the specific burden I am struggling to bear… brings peace.

The Holy Spirit is there to help us remember all that Jesus taught. He reminds us that God comforts the brokenhearted (Matthew 5:4 NIV), speaks for us when we cannot find the words (Romans 8:26 NIV), guides us (John 16:13 NIV), and holds us up (Psalm 63:8 NIV).

Jesus does not give as the world gives. Jesus gives us *peace.*

How is your heart troubled or afraid today? In what situation would you like to ask the Holy Spirit to be your helper? As you look for peace this Advent season, allow Him to be your comforter, advocate, intercessor, counselor, and strengthener. Bring your restless heart to Jesus and let him give you PEACE.

WEEK TWO: PEACE
Saturday

Follow After Peace

THIS WEEK WE have reflected on God's assurances of peace... The Holy Spirit provides peace that surpasses all understanding. The Lord reigns over all as the Prince of Peace. Our Father clothes us with peace. Jesus promises that He will give us peace. He himself is our peace.

So why do we still struggle to find peace?

Even though God renews us every day through his Holy Spirit, we tend to (time and time again) fall back into old ways and bad habits that rob us of peace.

FOLLOWING AFTER THE HOLY SPIRIT LEADS TO LIFE AND PEACE,
BUT FOLLOWING AFTER THE OLD NATURE LEADS TO DEATH.

– ROMANS 8:6 (TLB)

Following after the Holy Spirit leads to peace. *Following after* the old nature leads to death. The key question we need to ask ourselves is… *What (or who) are we following?*

During the Christmas season, in particular, our old nature can point us in the wrong direction. We find ourselves driven to shop, spend, and stress out… instead of rest, reflect, and renew.

As we take time to purposefully pursue peace this Advent season, we need to intentionally walk away from our old nature. Maybe that old self holds on to unforgiveness, is jealous of others' abilities to give, or envies the gifts others receive. It's hard to admit these things, but when we are honest with ourselves and acknowledge the areas where we struggle, we are one step closer to peace.

The next step is to *follow after* the Holy Spirit. In order to find peace, we need to let go of those bad habits and then *change direction*. We need to let our hearts be utterly transformed by God. I encourage you to follow after the Spirit that leads to peace today, by taking time to *rest, reflect, and renew.*

First, take time to *rest*. Peace comes in the quiet. The Holy Spirit wants to teach and instruct us, but we need to be listening. We need to allow both time and space to hear from God.

Then, *reflect*. Ask yourself… *What (or who) am I following?* Dig deep and determine if there are old habits that are robbing you of life and peace. Then try to pinpoint one specific part of your "old nature" that you want to eliminate—particularly in light of Christmas. Maybe it is anger from the past that draws you away from peace and healing during this time. Maybe it is selfishness that keeps you from serving others. Maybe it is overindulgence. Be specific, write it down, and make a choice not to "follow after" that part of your old nature anymore.

Then, *renew*. Replace that old habit with a good one. Spend time in prayer asking the Holy Spirit to lead and strengthen you. Refresh yourself by reading the Bible. If you are struggling with addiction, or anger, or something else of your "old nature" that is keeping you from God's peace, ask a friend to support you as you choose to walk a new path.

God wants you to have an *abundant* life… one that brings you hope, joy, love and PEACE. Today, and each day this Advent season, choose to let go of your old nature and, instead, follow after the Holy Spirit that leads to that life and PEACE.

Week Three: JOY

Choose Joy

The joy of the Lord is your strength!

NEHEMIAH 8:10 (ESV)

WEEK THREE: JOY
Sunday

Good News of Great Joy

HAPPINESS IS NOT the same as JOY.

Happiness is fleeting. It comes and goes. It may be captured for a moment, but then is quickly lost.

Joy is constant. It can stay with us through life's ups and downs. Author Kay Warren defines joy as "the settled assurance that God is in control of all the details of my life, the quiet confidence that ultimately everything is going to be alright, and the determined choice to praise God in every situation."[5]

A friend once shared with me this simple reminder—Our *happiness* is based on what is *happening*, but *joy* can be present *regardless of our circumstances.*

At Christmastime, there are many things that make us happy… gift giving, gift receiving, celebrations, baking (and eating!), and time well spent with family and friends. However, this week, I want to spend time reflecting on ways that we can *choose joy in every situation* (not just find moments of happiness).

> AND IN THE SAME REGION THERE WERE
> SHEPHERDS OUT IN THE FIELD,
> KEEPING WATCH OVER THEIR FLOCK BY NIGHT.
> AND AN ANGEL OF THE LORD APPEARED TO THEM,
> AND THE GLORY OF THE LORD SHONE AROUND THEM,
> AND THEY WERE FILLED WITH GREAT FEAR.
> AND THE ANGEL SAID TO THEM, "FEAR NOT, FOR BEHOLD,
> I BRING YOU GOOD NEWS OF GREAT JOY
> THAT WILL BE FOR ALL THE PEOPLE.
> FOR UNTO YOU IS BORN THIS DAY IN THE
> CITY OF DAVID A SAVIOR,
> WHO IS CHRIST THE LORD."
>
> – LUKE 2:8-11 (ESV)

The angels brought news of great joy that first Christmas when Jesus was born. I find two things remarkable about this joy…

First, the GOOD NEWS brings joy.

What was the good news? The news was that Christ, the Messiah, the Savior had finally arrived. These words would have been the fulfillment of lifelong hopes of these Jewish shepherds. For centuries, they had been expecting God to come and save them. The one they had been waiting for had just been born! This is more than just a one-time event to give them fleeting happiness. This is *hope fulfilled*.

Maybe there's something that you have hoped for over a long period of time—not just days, but months or even years or generations? A college acceptance. A dream job. A home. A child. A healing. A reconciliation. A relationship.

Do you remember the feeling you had when you realized the time had finally come? A mix of great anticipation, relief, and JOY!

This was what the shepherds must have been feeling after years of prophecy were *finally* being fulfilled. This was good news for them, and it is good news for us, too. Jesus came to save us.

Second, this joy is for ALL THE PEOPLE.

God did not just send his son to the Jewish nation. This good news is for *everyone*. Because when Jesus would later die on the cross, it would be for all of His creation.

And today, we can receive that joy wherever we are, whatever the circumstances. We can choose joy—by choosing Jesus—today.

There are so many choices we have to make during this season. I encourage you to think of three things you can do that will make you *happy*. Off the top of my head, walking around our neighborhood to see the Christmas lights, making monkey bread, and watching *It's a Wonderful Life* are on my list. I hope your holiday schedule allows you to enjoy some of the things that will make you *happy*!

Then, I encourage you to think of three ways that Jesus can bring you JOY this season where you most need it. His forgiveness, love, and peace are a few ideas to get you started. These things are always available and unchanging. They can seep deep into our lives no matter the circumstances.

As we begin this third week of Advent, may you rejoice knowing that the angels brought good news for the shepherds and for all of us. The waiting is over. A Savior has been born!

WEEK THREE: JOY
Monday

Sing for Joy

OH COME, LET US SING TO THE LORD;
LET US MAKE A JOYFUL NOISE TO THE
ROCK OF OUR SALVATION!
LET US COME INTO HIS PRESENCE WITH THANKSGIVING;
LET US MAKE A JOYFUL NOISE TO HIM WITH SONGS OF PRAISE!

– PSALM 95:1-2 (ESV)

THERE IS THE old adage of the chicken and the egg. Which came first?

Today, I ask the same question of SINGING and JOY… Which comes first?

I know that when I have an overwhelming sense of joy, it makes me want to sing. And I know that when I feel like I cannot find joy, a song can lift my weary soul.

I'm not sure which camp you are in today… whether you are searching for joy in this hectic season or overflowing with joy and "the Christmas spirit." But I know that joy is accessible to you, and I'm also confident that music is one path to experiencing that joy.

Singing is found throughout the Bible. King David sang songs of both lament and praise. The disciples sang with Jesus at the Passover supper. Paul and Silas sang hymns from their jail cell.

The soundtrack of our Christmas is carols. There are so many wonderful songs that speak of the JOY of Jesus' birth…

> *Joy to the world! The Lord has come!*
>
> *Oh come, all ye faithful, joyful and triumphant!*
>
> *Joyful, joyful, we adore thee!*
>
> *New life, new hope, new joy He brings*
> *Won't you listen to the angels sing?*
>
> *Angels we have heard on high, sweetly singing o'er the plains*
> *And the mountains in reply, echoing their joyous strains*[6]

Sometimes when songs are too familiar (and many carols are), we forget to reflect on the meaning of the words. So, I encourage you, as you listen to carols while you are cooking in the kitchen or driving in your car or out running errands, to hear the powerful words that tell the story of Jesus coming to the world. If you are struggling to find joy this Advent season, allow those songs to lead you back to the source of our JOY. And if you are already overflowing with joy, use those songs to make a joyful noise of praise!

WEEK THREE: JOY
Tuesday

Finding Joy

MY SON LIKES to hunt for treasure. He has since he was a little boy. He has gone through several metal detectors, countless shovels, and one "fishing magnet." (Look it up on YouTube.) He has scoured beaches, playgrounds, miles of walking paths and, of course, our own backyard. His "treasures" have included bottle caps, quarters, countless rusty nails, and a mailbox. (Don't ask.)

Despite their lack of monetary value, finding these things made my son so happy! I can only imagine his reaction if he came across real gold!

There is a parable in the book of Mark about a man who finds valuable treasure in a field…

"THE KINGDOM OF HEAVEN IS LIKE TREASURE
HIDDEN IN A FIELD.

WHEN A MAN FOUND IT, HE HID IT AGAIN,
AND THEN IN HIS JOY WENT AND SOLD ALL
HE HAD AND BOUGHT THAT FIELD."

– MATTHEW 13:44 (NIV)

The treasure this man found was "the kingdom of heaven" and, upon discovering it, he is filled with so much JOY that he sells everything he owns in order to obtain the lot on which it is buried.

I am struck by two things in this story…

First, "the kingdom of heaven"—life with Jesus, both now and in eternity—is a valuable treasure that brings us joy.

Second, sometimes we have to let go of what we already have in order to receive that treasure.

I am not suggesting that we need to literally sell all we have in order to follow Jesus. (Although some people may feel called to do this.) In fact, it is very clear throughout the Bible that we don't have to do anything to "earn" or "buy" a relationship with Jesus.

However, I think there are often things we hold onto (status, relationships, fear) that keep us from going "all in" on the treasure that can only be found in Him. Choosing to cling to these ultimately unsatisfying things robs us of the JOY of letting them go and embracing Jesus.

As you approach Christmas this year, perhaps you have a choice to make… Is there something you need to let go of in order to take hold of the treasure God has waiting for you? There is JOY waiting to be found!

WEEK THREE: JOY
Wednesday

Give Joyfully

CHRISTMAS IS A season of JOY. Unfortunately, one of the things that is meant to bring us joy at this time of year can actually rob us of our joy: gift-giving. The chaos of the mall, the stress of finding "the perfect gift," and the financial impact of buying so many gifts at once can take a toll on us. It can make it difficult to be a "cheerful giver."

EVERYONE MUST MAKE UP HIS OWN MIND
AS TO HOW MUCH HE SHOULD GIVE.
DON'T FORCE ANYONE TO GIVE MORE THAN HE REALLY WANTS TO,
FOR CHEERFUL GIVERS ARE THE ONES GOD PRIZES.
GOD IS ABLE TO MAKE IT UP TO YOU BY GIVING YOU
EVERYTHING YOU NEED AND MORE
SO THAT THERE WILL NOT ONLY BE ENOUGH FOR YOUR OWN NEEDS
BUT PLENTY LEFT OVER TO GIVE JOYFULLY TO OTHERS.

– 2 CORINTHIANS 9:7-8 (TLB)

The encouragement here is to give freely, knowing that God will care for your needs as you care for the needs of others. And, quite honestly, Paul is saying not to even bother to give if you can't do it cheerfully. This particular passage is specifically talking about financial giving to the church, but I think we can apply it to our Christmas gift-giving too.

This week, I encourage you to consider how you might reframe your thinking on gift-giving so the searching, spending, or sacrificing does not rob you of your joy this holiday season. There are a few ways we can keep our giving joy-filled...

1 – Pray purposefully.
2 – Budget realistically.
3 – Think creatively.

Start by praying purposefully. Cheerful gift-giving takes a bit of planning, and this best begins with prayer. Before you even start to shop, strategize, or create... ask God to give you insight as to how you might bless each person on your Christmas list. Ask for inspiration and ideation. You can also pray that every person is blessed with the incomparable gifts of hope, peace, joy and love this Advent season!

Then, come up with a realistic budget. While you may not think that budgets are biblical, the passage here explicitly guides everyone to "make up his [or her] own mind as to how much he [or she] should give." So, plan in advance. Decide what you are comfortable spending, then stick with it, so you can give cheerfully.

Finally, think creatively. One thing I have found helpful is to consider unique gifts that have deeper meaning and build greater connection, instead of gifts that can be bought at a store. I encourage you to contemplate how you might give a gift this year that is out-of-the-box (pun intended).

There are so many wonderful presents that cannot be purchased from store shelves! Maybe God has given you a special talent you can share by making personal Christmas gifts this year. Maybe you have skills and knowledge to impart. Perhaps you can offer to upgrade a niece or nephew's room by painting it with them, or clean out a grandparent's garage, or teach a practical skill like fishing or surfing or sewing to a friend or family member. Maybe the most precious offering you can give is quality time. Coupons for coffee dates and arrangements for other adventures can increase your joy not only on Christmas morning, but in the year ahead as you spend time investing in people you love!

Christmas is just around the corner, so take a little bit of time today to do some gift planning. Stop and consider how you might approach giving differently this year. Let God guide you toward out-of-the-box gift ideas that will bless those you love. And when your praying, budgeting, and creative brainstorming are done... give generously, give cheerfully, and give JOYFULLY.

WEEK THREE: JOY
Thursday

Joy in Trials

WHERE DO YOU find JOY at Christmas?

Do you find it in the warmth of a hug? Or the glow of the Christmas lights? Or the packages under the tree? Or the lyrics of a song?

Or... do you find it in your trials?

> COUNT IT ALL JOY, MY BROTHERS,
> WHEN YOU MEET TRIALS OF VARIOUS KINDS,
> FOR YOU KNOW THAT THE TESTING OF YOUR FAITH
> PRODUCES STEADFASTNESS.
> AND LET STEADFASTNESS HAVE ITS FULL EFFECT,
> THAT YOU MAY BE PERFECT AND COMPLETE,
> LACKING IN NOTHING.
>
> – JAMES 1:2-4 (ESV)

In the book of James, we read that we should respond with joy when we come across trials. (Umm… No, thank you.)

But as we keep reading, we are encouraged to consider trials joy because we *know*—that means we can be confident—those trials produce *steadfastness*. (This word is also sometimes translated as *patience*—which is not one of my stronger qualities.) And that steadfastness (patience) brings us closer to being perfect and complete.

Perhaps this Christmas season you feel overburdened, overwhelmed, unqualified or unprepared. It might be that you are facing "trials of various kinds," and you are struggling to find joy in the midst of them.

Hard circumstances have a way of stealing our joy. When we focus on what's going on around us, we are understandably discouraged. We need to *choose joy* and allow God to work in us while we work through difficulties. We have to intentionally set our eyes a bit down the road.

I want to encourage you… These trials are growing you. These trials are producing patience (a fruit of the Spirit!) in you. These trials are refining you and *perfecting* you. Whatever you feel that you are lacking, God will provide for you. His plan is for you to be made *complete* in Him.

If you are currently struggling through a difficult trial that is making it hard for you to find joy, I encourage you to pray this prayer today…

God, help me to find joy in this trial. Show me that you are with me. Give me the courage to get through this season and come out stronger on the other side. Please fill in the gaps where I'm lacking and grow me toward completion in You. Allow me to experience the joy that only you can bring this Christmas season.

God sees you in your struggle and knows the growth that it will bring… just as a plant pushes through the rocks and soil to blossom. May you choose JOY in knowing that something beautiful will come from the challenges you are facing.

WEEK THREE: JOY
Friday

Be Joyful Always

SINCE THE DAY she was born, I've had the words of 1 Thessalonians 5:16-18 on my daughter's wall…

> BE JOYFUL ALWAYS; PRAY CONTINUALLY;
> GIVE THANKS IN ALL CIRCUMSTANCES,
> FOR THIS IS GOD'S WILL FOR YOU IN CHRIST JESUS.
>
> – 1 THESSALONIANS 5:16-18 (NIV[7])

Be joyful always.

Really? *Always?* Keeping in mind that joy is not about our circumstances, being joyful always should be possible. However, having JOY all of the time still seems like a tall order.

But I think the secret to having a round-the-clock joy is to be found in the verses that follow…

Pray continually.

When I read this verse, I picture a monk, alone, undistracted, unaffected by worldly happenings (kids screaming), possessions (bills that need to be paid), or people (relationship drama). I'm a realist... that will never be me.

However, I can acknowledge that my prayer life always needs to be, and can be, expanded.

With good intentions, many of us pray at set times during the day... as we wake, when we share a meal, or before we lay our head on our pillow at night. These times of routine prayer are wonderful. The consistency and the ritual are important. Yet I think the calling here is, instead, to be in *an ongoing conversation* with God... constantly and conscientiously aware of His presence, and continually engaged with Him.

When we hear of the hurt of a friend, we say a quick prayer for him. When we see God moving in the world around us, we utter a breath of praise. When we are tired and struggling, we let out a cry for strength and mercy. When we are reminded of a gift we've been given, we give thanks at that moment.

Give thanks in all circumstances.

Have you ever noticed that the joyful people are the thankful people? The themes of joy and gratitude seem to go hand in hand.

It's not easy to muster up joy when you are not feeling it. But if you find yourself in that situation today, I urge you to give thanks. Right now. *Write now.* Make a list of ten things that you are thankful for. And let your heart and your mind be focused on those things.

As you refocus your eyes on the good gifts God has given you... in His creation, relationships, and His own Son... let thankfulness turn to joy that permeates deep into your heart.

For this is God's will for you in Christ Jesus.

God desires these things for us... that we would have JOY (and have it abundantly), that we would be in constant communication with Him, that we would be thankful for all that we've been given and all that He has done for us.

Today, rest in this... God wants to give you the gift of JOY throughout this Christmas season. Choose to take time during these busy days to talk with Him and to thank Him—and may your joy increase to overflowing!

WEEK THREE: JOY
Saturday

Fear and Joy

AT THE BEGINNING of this week, we read about the angels visiting the shepherds to announce the good news of great JOY that Christ had been born. As we come to the end of this week, we find an angel again bringing news of joy…

THE ANGEL SAID TO THE WOMEN, "DO NOT BE AFRAID,
FOR I KNOW THAT YOU ARE LOOKING FOR JESUS, WHO WAS CRUCIFIED.
HE IS NOT HERE; HE HAS RISEN, JUST AS HE SAID.
COME AND SEE THE PLACE WHERE HE LAY.
THEN GO QUICKLY AND TELL HIS DISCIPLES:
'HE HAS RISEN FROM THE DEAD
AND IS GOING AHEAD OF YOU INTO GALILEE.
THERE YOU WILL SEE HIM.' NOW I HAVE TOLD YOU."
SO THE WOMEN HURRIED AWAY FROM THE TOMB,
AFRAID YET FILLED WITH JOY,
AND RAN TO TELL HIS DISCIPLES.

– MATTHEW 28:5-8 (NIV)

Picture yourself as one of the women going to the tomb, carrying the spices you would use to anoint the body of Jesus, who had been crucified. Imagine the confusion and disappointment and sorrow they felt on their journey. Just weeks before, they thought that Jesus had come to free them and all of Israel from their Roman oppressors.

The Bible says that as they were walking to the tomb early that morning, they were pondering how they would even be able to roll away the heavy stone covering the entrance. But when they finally looked up, they saw that the stone had already been rolled away from the tomb.[8]

And there the angel told them that Christ had risen, *just as he said.*

And then we read a curious thing… The women were simultaneously *afraid yet filled with joy.*

We do not know why they were afraid… perhaps seeing the angel was terrifying… perhaps they couldn't get their heads around the fact that Jesus had risen from the dead… perhaps they were just scared because, even though they just received amazing news, they did not know exactly what would come next.

We are often walking that same road. There are many times when life is confusing and God's plan is not clear. Sometimes we don't feel like He is going to come through on His promises. Or we are distracted by what seems like an insurmountable roadblock. (Who is going to roll the stone away?) Or we just feel uncertain about *how* God will come through, even as we trust in Him.

There are times we feel unsure and fearful, but we need to remember that He will do *just as he said*...

> *I will strengthen you, I will help you.* (Isaiah 41:10 ESV)
> *I will counsel you with my eye upon you.* (Psalm 32:8 ESV)
> *I will never leave you nor forsake you.* (Hebrews 13:5 ESV)
> *I will give you rest.* (Matthew 11:28 ESV)
> *I am with you always.* (Matthew 28:20 ESV)

In spite of our fear, we can be filled with great JOY as we trust in the One who always keeps His word. What assurance do you need to cling to today, so that you might have joy in the midst of being afraid? I encourage you to circle one of the verses above and claim it as your own.

I pray that, no matter what uncertainty you are facing this Advent season, you will also have JOY, knowing that God will keep His promises, just as He said.

Week Four: LOVE

Love and Be Loved

May your roots go down deep into the soil of God's marvelous love; and may you be able to feel and understand, as all God's children should, how long, how wide, how deep, and how high his love really is; and to experience this love for yourselves.

Ephesians 3:17-19 (TLB)

WEEK FOUR: LOVE
Sunday

*If today is December 25th, turn to the special
CHRISTMAS DAY reading found at the end of this week.*

God Is Love

ONE OF MY favorite songs this time of year is Shawn Colvin's soothing version of "Love Came Down at Christmas."

> *Love came down at Christmas,*
> *Love all lovely, Love divine;*
> *Love was born at Christmas,*
> *Star and angels gave the sign.*[9]

Love literally came down at Christmas. It says in the Bible that God *is* love… so when He was born, love in bodily form appeared on earth.

AND SO WE KNOW AND RELY ON THE LOVE GOD HAS FOR US.
GOD IS LOVE.

– 1 JOHN 4:16 (NIV)

And what is love? We read in 1 Corinthians 13 (NIV) that…

Love is patient.

Love is kind.

Love does not envy.

Love does not boast.

Love is not proud.

Love does not dishonor others.

Love is not self-seeking.

Love is not easily angered.

Love keeps no record of wrongs.

Love does not delight in evil (but rejoices with the truth).

Love always protects.

Love always trusts.

Love always hopes.

Love always perseveres.

Love never fails.

As I have read through this summarization over the years, I have often felt that I'm being given an excellent example of how to love… but also a goal that is unattainable. We all know our own shortcomings too well to be able to live out the 1 Corinthians 13 definition of love perfectly. These are good attributes to work toward, but impossible to carry out on our own.

However, knowing that *God is love*, we can look at this through a different lens. We can have confidence that…

God is patient.

God is kind.

God does not envy.

God does not boast.

God is not proud.

God does not dishonor others.

God is not self-seeking.

God is not easily angered.

God keeps no record of wrongs.

God does not delight in evil (but rejoices with the truth).

God always protects.

God always trusts.

God always hopes.

God always perseveres.

God never fails.

We can know that God's PERFECT love will never fail us, even when we fail as we try to love others (or others fail as they try to love us).

Today... I encourage you to look at these two lists again as you think about God's love. Consider how you *are loved* and how you *can love others* as God loves you.

First, read again about who God is and choose one truth that you need to hear today. Underline it. Be confident that God is true to his character and loves *you* with the kindness, truth or perseverance you are longing for.

Then, read again about how we are called to LOVE and choose one way you are going to specifically extend God's love to someone else today.

WEEK FOUR: LOVE
Monday

If today is December 25th, turn to the special
CHRISTMAS DAY reading found at the end of this week.

The Fruit of the Spirit Is Love

IN THE BOOK of Galatians, there is an inventory of the fruit of the Spirit. And right there at the top of the list is LOVE…

> BUT THE FRUIT OF THE SPIRIT IS LOVE, JOY, PEACE, PATIENCE, KINDNESS, GOODNESS, FAITHFULNESS, GENTLENESS, SELF-CONTROL; AGAINST SUCH THINGS THERE IS NO LAW.
>
> – GALATIANS 5:22-23 (ESV)

What does it mean to have the "fruit of the Spirit" in our lives?

Just as we see and enjoy the good fruit of a flourishing tree in the physical world, a person in a healthy relationship with God should show and share these qualities, led first and foremost by love. As with all good relationships, some of this growth is because of the work we put into it, and some of it is because of the generous contributions of the other party.

It is clear that fruit is EVIDENCE of the Holy Spirit working in a person's life... something that naturally flows from a person who is following Jesus. We know God has lavished love upon us (1 John 3:1 NIV), surrounds us with a shield of love (Psalm 5:12 NLT), and that His love is poured into our hearts when we believe in Him (Romans 5:5 NIV). These outpourings of love are initiated by God and, when we accept them, naturally continue to bear the fruit of love in our lives.

Yet it is also a CHOICE to bear fruit... selecting the path of love, joy, peace, and so on, as various circumstances come our way—and those choices draw us closer to Jesus. In the verses just before this passage, the apostle Paul advises us to WALK by the Spirit (Galatians 5:16 ESV) and BE LED by the Spirit (Galatians 5:18 ESV). These are clear commands for us to make decisions to seek God and his direction and strength *in order to* love others. "Walking" and "being led" may come through quiet prayer and meditation, reading the Bible, or seeking wise counsel when we struggle to act in love.

It seems to be a continuous cycle—God pours out His love on us... then we choose to walk in love... which draws us closer to God... which makes it easier to love... which brings us closer to God... which allows His love to flow through us...

Today, I encourage you to consider where you can jump into the cycle.

Is there something in your life that is preventing you from receiving and accepting God's love? Take time this Christmas to reflect on the story of God's great love for you, so much that He sent His son to be born in a manger.

Or, is there an area where you have not been choosing to love others? Thinking back on the characteristics of God's love we read in 1 Corinthians 13.... How can you love with more patience, kindness, humility or hope? What steps can you take this Christmas to be filled and led by the Holy Spirit in order to share the love that He has already shared with you?

Let LOVE—a fruit of the Spirit—grow abundantly in your life this Christmas season!

WEEK FOUR: LOVE
Tuesday

If today is December 25th, turn to the special
CHRISTMAS DAY reading found at the end of this week.

Love Leads to Forgiveness

AS WE CONSIDER how to love and how much we are loved, we should also contemplate how we can forgive, just as we are forgiven.

GOD HAS CHOSEN YOU AND MADE YOU HIS HOLY PEOPLE.
HE LOVES YOU.
SO YOU SHOULD ALWAYS CLOTHE YOURSELVES WITH MERCY,
KINDNESS, HUMILITY, GENTLENESS, AND PATIENCE.
BEAR WITH EACH OTHER, AND FORGIVE EACH OTHER.
IF SOMEONE DOES WRONG TO YOU,
FORGIVE THAT PERSON BECAUSE THE LORD FORGAVE YOU.
EVEN MORE THAN ALL THIS, CLOTHE YOURSELF IN LOVE.
LOVE IS WHAT HOLDS YOU ALL TOGETHER IN PERFECT UNITY.

– COLOSSIANS 3:12-14 (NCV)

When my kids were young, we moved to England for a few years, and they both attended a local British school, where they wore uniforms every day. As part of a school chapel lesson one afternoon, I shared these verses with the students and they each decorated hangers for their blazers with the adjectives hanging from colorful strands of yarn. This was meant to be a reminder that, as they literally dressed themselves in the morning, they should also clothe themselves with these loving attitudes.

The brief list of traits in Colossians 3 includes: mercy, kindness, humility, gentleness and patience. We've seen these words before in the long record of attributes of love in 1 Corinthians and the fruit of the Spirit in Galatians 5. Here, though, the author (Paul the apostle) goes on to say exactly why we need to clothe ourselves with these things—so that we can forgive: "Bear with each other, and forgive each other. If someone does wrong to you, forgive that person *because the Lord forgave you*." (Colossians 3:13 NCV)

Part of loving others is forgiving them.

Sometimes forgiveness is not that hard. A child breaks a favorite knick-knack, but you know that it was an accident. A friend is late for a coffee date and, although you were not happy about the awkward time you sat alone, you easily let it go once you begin to enjoy your time together.

Other times, though, forgiveness does not come so easily. Someone may have wronged you in a way that was intentional, physically painful, or irreparable. What do we do in those situations? We are still gently asked to forgive, just as God has forgiven us. This forgiveness does not dismiss the hurtful actions or absolve the other party of due consequences, but it does help us to let go of the resentment that takes up space in our heart and allows healing to begin.

We have all made choices in our life that require us to ask for forgiveness... from family, from friends, and from God. And Jesus' response is always to forgive because of His great love for us. And when we forgive others—as He forgives us—that love can cover all of the hurt, wounds or damage someone may have caused.

This Christmas, you may be holding on to resentment or unforgiveness. Perhaps it's for something small... your partner didn't take care of a holiday errand, your sibling won't host the family gathering this year, or you were not invited to a friend's party. Perhaps it's for something larger that has been with you for years... deep hurt over a lost relationship, the wound from broken trust, or other painful memories. Whichever the case may be, I encourage you to start the process of healing today by taking your pain to God and simply asking him to start you on the road to forgiveness by softening your heart to prepare you to forgive.

Choosing forgiveness is choosing to clothe yourself in LOVE. And again, "putting on" a love that holds this all together is a beautiful image. If we have a wardrobe of mercy, humility, and patience, I imagine that love is a fantastic cloak. It's that final piece of clothing that offers warmth and protection. It holds us all together as we wrestle through offering forgiveness to one another. May you feel that love covering you today as you forgive others, as you have been forgiven.

WEEK FOUR: LOVE
Wednesday

*If today is December 25th, turn to the special
CHRISTMAS DAY reading found at the end of this week.*

Unconditional Love

ROMANS 8 TELLS us we should be confident that *nothing* can separate us from God's love…

FOR I AM CONVINCED THAT NEITHER DEATH NOR LIFE,

NEITHER ANGELS NOR DEMONS,

NEITHER THE PRESENT NOR THE FUTURE,

NOR ANY POWERS,

NEITHER HEIGHT NOR DEPTH,

NOR ANYTHING ELSE IN ALL CREATION,

WILL BE ABLE TO SEPARATE US FROM THE LOVE OF GOD

THAT IS IN CHRIST JESUS OUR LORD.

— ROMANS 8:38-39 (NIV)

With talk of such immense circumstances as life and death, angels and demons, and past and present, we immediately think that this verse is only about major events in our lives—an irreversible mistake in judgement, incapacitating illness, extreme hardships.

And it is true… none of these can keep us from the unconditional love of God.

However, I think it can be the small things that creep in, even the seemingly good things, that pull us away from His love during the Christmas season.

One of the reasons that I have become so attached to Advent—and taking time to reflect on God's hope, peace, joy and love during this season—is because I have repeatedly found that some of the traditional activities we most closely associate with Christmas (family gatherings, decorating, gift-giving, even serving) become the very things that distract us from Jesus.

We can become so enamored with the *atmosphere* of Christmas—the sights, smells, and tastes—that when those things are lacking (which inevitably, in some circumstance or another during the busy holidays, they are), we do not *feel* the love that is meant to be so prevalent at this time of year.

Our time and energy can also become so focused on preparing our home for guests, the details of our child's school party, or the office secret Santa exchange that we become stressed and frayed. And, dare I say, we may sometimes think that our over-the-top performance in these activities will earn us the love of family, friends, or co-workers.

While our actions may gain us favor with some, they are not the reason God loves us.

As I read Romans 8, and am reminded of God's unrelenting, immeasurable love for us through all of the difficulties we may face in life, I can also confidently say that…

Neither long lines nor empty shelves…
Neither poorly shaped Christmas trees nor burnt out twinkle lights…
Neither gifts that don't arrive on time nor crafts that aren't completed…
Neither unfinished gingerbread houses nor unopened Advent calendars…
… can separate us from God's love.

You may laugh, but sometimes it is these little frustrations that draw us away from Him, and from loving others well, as we prepare to celebrate Christmas. We forget that our decorations, our cooking, and our gifts are not tied to His love for us… and the lack of them does not take away from it either.

This Christmas, may you embrace all of your festivities with joy. Let your traditions and celebrations allow you to fully love others and also draw you close to the God who loves you. And if one (or many!) of the little things do not go as planned, know that He is still right there. May you remain confident during this busy Advent season that there is nothing (big or small) that can separate you from God's LOVE.

WEEK FOUR: LOVE
Thursday
*If today is December 25th, turn to the special
CHRISTMAS DAY reading found at the end of this week.*

Love God, Yourself & Others

SOMEONE ONCE ASKED Jesus which is the most important commandment, and this was his reply…

> "'LOVE THE LORD YOUR GOD WITH ALL YOUR HEART
> AND WITH ALL YOUR SOUL
> AND WITH ALL YOUR MIND AND WITH ALL YOUR STRENGTH.'
> THE SECOND IS THIS: 'LOVE YOUR NEIGHBOR AS YOURSELF.'
> THERE IS NO COMMANDMENT GREATER THAN THESE."

> – MARK 12:30-31 (NIV)

In this passage, I feel like Jesus is giving us a pretty clear priority list on love:

1 – Love God.

2 – Love yourself.

3 – Love your neighbor.

The first part is fairly straightforward… Love God with ALL of your heart, soul, mind and strength.

Now, just because there is clear direction on this first point, it does not mean that this is an easy undertaking. Giving ourselves over to God in our entirety is no simple task, but I encourage you to examine which parts of yourself you are keeping from Him. The one who is asking for your whole heart wants to care for it with great tenderness!

The second part is often overlooked… Love your neighbor *as yourself.*

Have you considered that it might be difficult to love your neighbor if you don't love yourself first? We need to accept God's love if we are going to share it. If we are going to care for, forgive, and love others, we need to start by accepting God's care, forgiveness, and love; seeing ourselves through His eyes, and loving who He has made us to be.

Finally, we are also called to love others.

Even though this is the last directive on this list, it does not mean it is unimportant. We are consistently called to love one another. This often means time, sacrifice, and effort—and sometimes includes suffering and pain for the sake of another—which is why it is so important to be secure in God's love and to take care of ourselves if we want to do this one well!

As we focus on love this week, I encourage you to ask yourself these questions, with the priorities of loving God, loving yourself, and loving others in mind…

1 – What part of my life (my heart, soul, mind or strength) am I not sharing with God? How can I love Him more fully?

2 – What does it look like for me to love myself? In what area do I need to have the same grace for myself as God already has for me?

3 – What is one specific way I can love my neighbor (a good friend, an acquaintance, or even a stranger in need) during this Christmas season?

As we LOVE more fully… upwardly, inwardly, and outwardly… we will be blessed to both receive and share God's love.

WEEK FOUR: LOVE
Friday

If today is December 25th, turn to the special
CHRISTMAS DAY reading found at the end of this week.

Motivated by Love

1 CORINTHIANS 13 (one of the most quoted chapters in the Bible on the topic of love) opens with these words…

IF I SPEAK IN THE TONGUES OF MEN OR OF ANGELS,
BUT DO NOT HAVE LOVE,
I AM ONLY A RESOUNDING GONG OR A CLANGING CYMBAL.
IF I HAVE THE GIFT OF PROPHECY AND CAN FATHOM ALL
MYSTERIES AND ALL KNOWLEDGE,
AND IF I HAVE A FAITH THAT CAN MOVE MOUNTAINS,
BUT DO NOT HAVE LOVE, I AM NOTHING.
IF I GIVE ALL I POSSESS TO THE POOR
AND GIVE OVER MY BODY TO HARDSHIP THAT I MAY BOAST,
BUT DO NOT HAVE LOVE, I GAIN NOTHING.

— 1 CORINTHIANS 13:1-3 (NIV)

As we read through this passage, we find a list of amazing spiritual gifts—gifts that are meant to build up the church and care for others...

The ability to speak wisdom eloquently.
The faith to trust in God for miracles.
The desire to give generously.

But if we share any of these gifts without the right motive, they are hollow.

This passage is a not-so-gentle reminder that all that we do needs to be done in love. Let's keep that in mind as Christmas quickly approaches...

If we host the most elaborate parties, but are more concerned about the decorations than we are about our guests, we've given them nothing of value.

If we sing carols in the choir (or from the pew) with perfect pitch and tone, but our hearts are not worshipping God, we've given Him nothing of value.

If we give the most expensive presents, but without thought or care for the recipient, we've given the person nothing of value.

Because it's not just about *what* we do... *why* we share our gifts is also important. Our intentions matter.

Take this to heart. Today, if there is something that you are not looking forward to doing this Christmas season, ask yourself why you decided to undertake it in the first place. Sometimes it helps to stop and remember *why* we originally chose to participate and remember *who* we are loving through our efforts. Instead of being overwhelmed by the time commitments and the details, set your mind—and your heart—on the people who you are loving through your deeds. Often this will bring the joy back to the celebration.

However, there are also situations where we know that we are supposed to do something for the benefit of others, even when our feelings toward them have not caught up yet. In these times, we may need to set our eyes on Jesus as the one we are loving through our actions.

And a final thought... Perhaps there is an event you are expected to host, or an obligation that you feel responsible to carry, or an annual holiday activity that you can no longer do with an attitude of love. If that is the case, maybe it would be better to let it go. I can't imagine that it does anyone any good if the song of our lives is just a resounding gong or a clanging cymbal.

As we reflect on God's LOVE for us this week, let us remember to let that love be our motivation. Let our love—and His love—be the reason we throw the parties, sing the songs, and give the gifts we do!

WEEK FOUR: LOVE
Saturday

*If today is December 25th, turn to the special
CHRISTMAS DAY reading found at the end of this week.*

Love One Another

THERE IS A wonderful little children's book called <u>Have You Filled a Bucket Today?</u> This book contains a special nugget of truth:

> *You fill a bucket when you show love to someone, when you say or do something kind, or even when you give someone a smile...*

> *But guess what... when you fill someone else's bucket, you fill your own bucket, too.*[10]

It's a lovely guiding principle for pre-school kids (and still applies to us today)... Sometimes the best way to fill our own "love tank"[11] is to love others.

No one has ever seen God; but if we LOVE one another,
God lives in us and his love is made complete in us.

– 1 John 4:12 (NIV)

When we love others, God's love is made *complete* in us. It is not enough for us to receive God's love—we need to *respond* to it for it to come to full fruition!

I wholeheartedly believe that we need to be wary of doing too much during the Christmas season. I have stressed more than once over the last four weeks that our *doing* can be our *undoing*. As we seek hope, peace, joy, and love, we need to take time to reflect and pray so we don't take on burdens we are not meant to carry... and so we can receive the gifts God has for us.

However, as it is with most things in life, the mature approach does not usually sit at the extremes. While we are called to rest and reflect, we are also called to action. And so, while we must be cautious about trying to earn love through unhealthy self–sacrifice, we must also be willing to give love away—through kindness and service—in order to increase the love we hold in our hearts.

Jesus himself modeled how to love others when he washed the disciples' feet. This was not something He had to do. It was something He chose to do. He humbled himself and served them in this way and then He said:

"A new command I give you: LOVE one another.
As I have loved you, so you must love one another."

– John 13:34 (NIV)

You may feel depleted right now, empty, and unable to give anything… but God has already loved you. Through *His* love, you can love others. He may be asking you to pour out love to someone so that he can fill you to the brim!

I encourage you, as we approach Christmas Day, to make an offering to someone… a kind word, an invitation for a cup of coffee, an olive branch of forgiveness. Love others as you want to be loved. Love others as Jesus loves you. You might find that, by extending LOVE to others, God not only blesses them through you, but also fills your own bucket and brings you closer to fulfillment, maturity, and completion.

WEEK FOUR: LOVE
CHRISTMAS DAY

The Gift of Love

Jesus loves you.

MAYBE YOU'VE BEEN told this your whole life. Maybe you've never heard it before. Either way, I think that, sometimes, this simple phrase goes too easily in one ear and out the other.

Jesus loves you.

If you haven't heard this verse in church, you've probably seen it written on a sign in the stands at a football game:

> FOR GOD SO LOVED THE WORLD, THAT HE GAVE HIS
> ONE AND ONLY SON, THAT WHOEVER BELIEVES IN HIM
> SHOULD NOT PERISH BUT HAVE ETERNAL LIFE.
>
> – JOHN 3:16 (NIV)

This is what Christmas is all about, God's gift to YOU. With all the focus on giving to others, preparing for parties, and even going to church... don't miss this.

Jesus loves you.

He loves you right now. He loved you before you were born. He loved you through every mistake you've made. He will always love you, no matter what you do.

Jesus loves you.

Sometimes, when we reflect on Jesus' love for us, it's too abstract to wrap our minds around, so we use what we know to envision it... the love of a parent, the love of a best friend, the love of a spouse. But these are all imperfect. These cannot possibly compare to the grace-filled, all-encompassing, willing-to-die-for-you love of Jesus.

Jesus loves you.

Not in spite of who you are or what you've done, but because of who HE is and what He's done. He created you, then gave his life for you... knowing all along that you are not perfect and that life would be messy.

Jesus loves you.

Do not miss receiving this special gift for YOU this Christmas!

But God, being rich in mercy,
because of His great LOVE with which He loved us,
even when we were dead in sins,
made us alive together with Christ...
For by grace you have been saved through faith,
and this is not of yourselves
It is the gift of God.

– Ephesians 2:4-5, 8 (MEV)

EPILOGUE

Dear Reader,

I love the change of seasons.

When we lived in England, I loved to watch the seasons transform the landscape. Our house sat across the street from a little green, and there was one particularly large and magnificent tree that reflected the passing of time with its changing leaves, budding flowers, and dry branches.

Here in Southern California, most days are mild and sunny, and palm trees don't change very much. But, regardless of the weather, I am always ready for a new season every few months. Each summer, I am quick to throw off our regular schedules and embark on days-long adventures. By the fall, I crave the routine that my kids' school schedule brings. As the days grow short, I look forward to the Thanksgiving gatherings and preparations for Christmas. And by early spring, I yearn for the new life that blossoms all around us.

Advent is a season of preparation. It's a season I did not want you to miss, as you reflected on and celebrated Christmas.

But what is your next season? Perhaps some of you are looking forward to a great adventure in the year ahead! For others, the holidays can be hard, and the days following may be even harder.

Did you know that the Twelve Days of Christmas refers to the twelve days *after* Christmas? Christmastide, as it is also known, is the short season on the liturgical calendar from December 25 to January 5. I encourage you to embrace it and take these next twelve days to prepare for the new year.

Read the Bible. Pray. If Christmas Day came before you finished the week four devotionals, read through the remaining meditations about God's love.

Ask God what He has in store for you in the year ahead. What are His plans for you? Don't be overwhelmed by searching for too many answers, but listen and see if there is one thing, one phrase, or one word that you might focus on in the year ahead.

The hope, peace, joy and love that Christ offered at Christmas are not only held out to you for a few short weeks—they are meant to be taken and unwrapped and enjoyed all year through.

Merry Christmas and Happy New Year to you.

With love,
Jen

ACKNOWLEDGEMENTS

This has been quite a year. Honestly, if it were not for the global pandemic, I probably would never have sat down long enough to write this book. A significantly slowed work schedule and family calendar allowed me to pour into this project over twelve crazy months. What you are holding in your hands is my genuine silver lining.

Although it took about a year to put to paper, this project has been decades in the making.

It began with my own introduction to Advent when I was in college. While attending Malibu Presbyterian (now Malibu Pacific) Church, I first saw Advent candles lit on a Sunday morning and spent my own time reflecting on the season through a devotional written by the pastor's wife, Nancy Worth. Nancy, this book is a reflection of the exponential impact of your act of obedience.

From there, embracing Advent became a tradition in our home (as it had been in my husband's home the previous generation). In addition to celebrating the season with my own family, I have found myself encouraging others to slow down and enjoy the weeks leading up to Christmas. Years of sharing, songwriting, and speaking about Advent laid the groundwork for many of these devotions.

And so, during the 2020 Advent season, a small group of people were asked to be my first readers. I am incredibly thankful to the family, OCF friends, Bible study ladies, Friday morning prayer moms, and SLO Crew who gave me feedback on that first version. Thank you for your time, for reading and rating entries, and for being kind to my very rough draft.

As things shaped up in the New Year, I passed revised versions on to Erik Seversen and Dr. Brandon Cash. I am extremely grateful for the encouragement and feedback each of you gave to me. You affirmed thoughts I was not sure if I should include and brought helpful new ideas for writing, formatting, and publishing to my attention.

Through this whole process, my sweet husband brought his spiritual wisdom and B.A. in English to the table. He read every draft—Every. Single. Draft. He shared incredibly constructive insights and much-needed encouragement. John, I am completely aware that this never would have happened without your love and support.

As we spent almost every hour of every day together in our house over the last year, my teens blessed me with their patience and prayers. Lane and Ryan, I love you. Even though our family prayer time can get a little rowdy, I appreciate that I can share my heart with you and that you pray for me.

And, last but not least, I am grateful to Jesus—for the hope, peace, joy and love He freely gives. I am thankful that You are both my Savior and Friend. The words on these pages, I hope, stem from your Holy Spirit's leading. May they bring glory to You and You alone.

NOTES

1   James Strong, *The Exhaustive Concordance of the Bible* (McLean, MacDonald, 1991) 102.

2   Egan, William C. "Silent Night! Holy Night!," Silent Night Web, March 23, 2021, http://www.silentnight.web.za/translate/eng.htm.

3   2 Corinthians 13:11 (CEV)

4   John 14:26-27. The Amplified Bible: Containing the Amplified Old Testament and the Amplified New Testament. Grand Rapids, Mich: Zondervan Pub. House, 1965.

5   Kay Warren, *Choose Joy, Because Happiness Isn't Enough* (Grand Rapids, Revell, a division of Baker Publishing Group, 2012) 31.

6   Lyrics from "Joy to the World," "Oh Come All Ye Faithful," "Joyful Joyful We Adore Thee," "Jesus Oh What a Wonderful Child" and "Angels We Have Heard On High" are all public domain.

7   This translation is taken specifically from the *Holy Bible*, New International Version. Zondervan Publishing House, 1984.

8   Mark 16:1-4

9   "Love Came Down at Christmas" (Christina G. Rossetti, pub.1885)

10 Carol McCloud, *Have You Filled a Bucket Today?* (Northville, Nelson Publishing, 2008) 12, 17.

11 Gary Chapman coined the term "love tank" in his book, *The Five Love Languages* (Chicago, Northfield Publishing, 1992).